This book is dedicated to my parents, Al and Lana Edwards for their support, dedication and profound examples of leadership.

Beginning Your Wealth in Affordable Housing:
A Motivational Handbook

Contents

Introduction

After great reluctance and procrastination, I've finally decided, in my limited literary capacity, to write a brief, constructive account of my experience in real estate; specifically, the 1–4 family residential segment. While the title has an ambitious tone, the real purpose of this short script is to answer the many earnest inquiries I've received over the years about my foray into real estate investment. My reluctance is because I do not regard myself to be a considerable authority on many subjects, including real estate. I have, however, had a transformative economic experience with the vehicle of real estate at the fulcrum of it. I've managed, with the combination of study and determined effort, to build a portfolio of residential rental properties whose value and positive impact has exceeded my aims and expectations.

The term *real estate* is a mouthful. I remind myself that it describes every patch of land not covered by water as well as many others that are. Since it represents practically everything a human eye can see, it's essential that I clarify that this handbook covers only a tiny subset that I employed to begin my personal journey from financial obscurity to relative economic prominence. In the upcoming chapters, I will narrow the focus of this broad subject.

I also will confine my personal details only to those supportive of the techniques and disciplines that I believe are pertinent to the subject, for I do not wish for this book to be autobiographical nearly as much as educational. The only value in my personal accounts is in their demonstration of effectiveness of the information being put forth. I will use references to business publications that I utilized. Because I attribute a great deal of my success to the authors of personal-development material, I will leave a roadmap of these books and papers to you, the reader, and what I believe I've gained in the process of integrating their readings into my philosophy and efforts.

My hope is to answer the general question of how I achieved success in the field of real estate—at least in the segment I have worked in. I wish as well to demonstrate the dramatic difference it has made for me and how beneficial a shift from my prior path it has represented. Finally, I hope to provide tools useful to replicating and exceeding my own goals with a good chance of helping you achieve yours.

I must state in advance that this account may turn out to largely be a period piece. As I've gathered relevant accounts from the nineteen years of my investing experience, I've realized how some of the circumstances that gave rise to my results were unique or one-time events. As an investor in New Orleans, Louisiana, beginning in the 1990's, through the profound occurrence of Hurricane Katrina and the subsequent recovery, there are elements of my experience that are simply uncommon, so I will normalize my accounts for adaptation to predictable circumstances. I'll also make an effort to identify characteristics of the New Orleans area that exist in most American cities, making them conducive for successful investment in kind. It is also true that my beginnings were set in a far different regulatory and political environment than that which exists today. I pledge to identify some of those differences and give my best opinion on how to navigate the challenges that the present-day investor faces, though they may not have troubled us twenty years ago.

If done correctly, one half of this book will review what I did both well and poorly, along with some results. The other half will be a prognostication of what can work going forward and the initial steps supporting a simple strategy to begin building wealth. The critical first six to twelve months can either set a trajectory for optimism and success or a frustrating and perilous struggle. Property search, evaluation, selection, financing and even partnership strategy can make or break an investment endeavor and few sources I've found address these categories specific to affordable housing.

I hope to inject enough levity to freshen up the technical lecture segments, although they're essential. Collectively, however, I wish for this effort to serve as an affirmation to any potential investor to move ahead, confidently inspired by the story of a modestly prepared beginner who succeeded while learning on the job.

I'll regularly remind you that this is merely a guide to a good start and a reference to other more comprehensive texts on the important subcategories you will benefit from studying. Other technically based resources will go more heavily into intermediate levels of equity investing, of which real estate is but a single segment. My main goal is to be encouraging with my personal story while providing the tools necessary to get you going. I didn't know any really successful investors whom I could call upon to give me vital instruction, and I know how valuable that can be. I also know how empowering asset ownership can be and how a productive future depends on your investment efforts. Most importantly, I wish to lead you beyond the pitfalls of a disastrous beginning. I'd be thrilled to hear that someone has made successful strides while *not* making some of the avoidable mistakes I made along the way.

I caution that you will need more than this brief framework as an information source for a career in real estate investment. It stands to reason that a field so broad and lucrative should be rather involved, and this is but a brief handbook. I do hope to have this serve as the encouragement to explore and pursue residential investment property as a vehicle to wealth creation and prosperity.

Chapter 1

The Five *W*'s

I believe the 'who' also can be you.

I will begin with a brief background of my story so that references I make throughout the book have context. I hope to confine my personal platitudes to the first and last chapters, in which I'll be hammering home the point that real estate is a terrific pathway to wealth development, especially when starting from nothing. As with anything, however, it is more involved than it appears at a glance and can be intimidating in the absence of guidance. I wish for this book to provide the confidence to pursue your goals through real estate and to serve as the blueprint to a great start for you as well.

In journalism, the five *W*'s are the first essential questions asked for the purpose of building any story: **who**, **what**, **when**, **where**, and **why**?

I ask and will answer these questions based on the emphasis I think matters most. I suggest that you refer to these answers when building your strategy to attack your respective market or the area you wish to invest in. While some details may seem incidental, I believe that the presence or absence of some of these characteristics would have significantly affected my outcomes, had I known to give them thought back then. It's hard to tell how different circumstances might have affected decisions made along the way or their effectiveness, so these things may be very important.

The **who** is myself—Just a guy named Al who was about twenty-seven years old when I began pursuing my interest in real estate.

I had been on the premed track since childhood, having attended an allied health high school beginning at the age of thirteen. I had attended college in New Orleans following high school and earned an undergraduate degree in premedical biology. I wasn't a great student, but I was competent. I wasn't very inspired by my potential career path of medicine as a lab technician, teacher, physician, or anything else.

After suffering through a poorly suited curriculum of major courses and getting my degree, I took a couple of years off to just decompress and generally loaf about. I worked in unrelated random fields in my college town until an enterprising college buddy who had started a small retail operation sought out a partner to expand to a second location. The small-tobacco shop endeavor didn't require much money; just effort and a decent idea of things that might sell in the high-traffic area of the tourist district in New Orleans. I started a small kiosk with my new partner, and we had fun with the activity of operating a startup, more so that we made money, but we both considered it a success. I loved the experience of not being subject to oversight. It was very liberating and inspired me to work harder and longer, knowing that the fruit of my efforts would be my own. The effort didn't endure more than two years but served as the catalyst of my entrepreneurial interest and segue into real estate.

I was the child of two very successful and effective but very different parents. My mother was a career educator with a master's in English literature. She was such an influence on my communication skills that she even served as my official English teacher in the eleventh grade. My father, by contrast, was a General Foods warehouse lift truck operator turned Texas state representative and eventual member of *Who's Who Among Black Americans* as the author of important civil rights and equality legislation. My father had real disdain for entry-level employment and taking orders from others, while my mother was a very polished teacher/principal for forty-four years. My folks disagreed on the importance of higher education, as each had succeeded on either side of the proposition. Alas, my highest motivation for the pursuit of success was an embarrassing acquaintance with disrespect. I can laugh about it now, but hopefully, you'll be more self-motivated than I was! I'll speak about that later.

A great deal more has happened since my beginning in real estate back in 1999. Over the years, I've acquired a good deal more education, including an MBA and an FAA certification, but those things didn't contribute to my early success. In fact, the opportunities to grow and expand my knowledge were the product of my good start in real estate. The most relevant point is that I was not at all trained in real estate or construction. I had no college courses in economics, finance, or business, and I wasn't the product of a business-enterprising household. I didn't have two parents who saw high value in college education, although they both had degrees. I think my father saw his degree more as a qualifying document than a useful tool. My father was more of a "hard work" kind of guy, with a greater appreciation for physical labor and was not particularly motivated regarding real estate or entrepreneurship. I was able bodied and in good health. I was open to good counsel and willing to read at length about any techniques that would benefit me in my interest, but that was about it. That context should be encouraging for anyone in doubt about their capacity to do well in the ways that I have in real estate. I believe the **who** also can be you. If you're seeking introductory information on the subject, such as this beginner's book, you already have the most important ingredient: curiosity. I'd like to think that you'll turn that curiosity into productive step-taking.

The **what** is much more important. I am speaking of 1–4 family residential real estate as well as small commercial existing structures. There are specific reasons why in the beginning, with limited resources and no experience, these categories are so essential.

No one should have trusted me with financing a speculative construction real estate effort under the cash and credit constraints I began my career with. Existing structures are less speculative than attempting to build real estate for a potentially profitable sale. More importantly, the 1–4 family category allows for the versatility of financing via the Federal Housing Administration (FHA) or consumer and commercial means among traditional options. Secondary means of financing also find the abundance of the product type comforting. The time horizon of development and cash requirements are too high for a beginner to handle while still controlling a decent percentage of his or her deal. Unless you've worked closely or in a master capacity in construction trades, cost will eat you alive when efficiency is optimally important. You will want to acquire real estate that you can infuse with your own sweat equity and be able to afford to acquire with reasonable investment assistance and expectations. Existing structures offer a much shorter time frame for solvency and completing a project. I will get further into these details later.

The 1–4 family market is very easy to understand. With over 136 million residential units in the United States,[1] banks and outside investors alike find the segment easy to get comfortable with. Valuations are relatively durable and predictable with plenty of comparable-value information available. The great value in this real estate product is that it lets the owner lease the property for either partial owner occupancy or non owner occupancy for long-term ownership.

Another of the great advents of the small-rental property market is the technology evolution's impact on the vacation rental industry. Of course, absolutely everything is now sold or has a cyber-retail presence online. Airbnb and Vrbo, which concentrate on vacation rentals, have created a submarket in competition with the hotel industry that is ideal for 1–4 family residential real estate. Part of my strategy has been to have as many available outlets for my investment product as possible. With the ability to occupy, lease long term, sell as improved, or operate as a quasi-hotel, this versatility gives you the greatest financial protection in adverse market conditions. This industry is early in its development as of 2019, and municipalities are frequently modifying legislation to prevent abuse of the platform. As you might imagine, the

---

[1]Statista. "Number of Housing Units in the United States from 1975 to 2018 (In Millions)." Unknown. Accessed August 14, 2019. https://www.statista.com/statistics/240267/number-of-housing-units-in-the-united-states/.

hotel industry heavily opposes the vacation rental market, so be careful how you make long-term investment decisions based on regulations that are still in flux. Still, the more outlets for your product at their most financially vulnerable stage, the better! I'll expand my discussion on the **what** and its characteristics at other points as well.

The **when** is what I would call a dual question, so I'll answer it twice. First, without being too platitudinous, *right now*! There's no better time to put this type of investment mechanism in place. Time is your ally in real estate investment, as you stand to enjoy value appreciation and residual cash flow on lease and rental revenue. There is some strategy in the timing of buying certain properties where exogenous factors in the neighborhood may dramatically raise or lower value over a short time. In a prospecting segment, we will cover more details surrounding timing and cyclical annual periods, but at the beginning, global economic   influences will be few.

The thing to remember is that the earlier you own income property, the sooner you will begin building your track record as an investor as well as your real level of experience. Historically, US real estate values appreciate very efficiently in conjunction with the growth of the gross domestic product (GDP). The sooner you own property in areas you're familiar and comfortable with, the more that appreciation can take place under *your* ownership! I make the comparison between investment real estate ownership and the possession of education. The later you acquire your education, the less of your life you have to use it because it perishes with you. Similarly, the later you acquire real estate, the more it likely appreciates outside of your ownership. You benefit most greatly from value appreciation; a concept I will expand on later.

The second answer is sort of an underlying answer I alluded to in mentioning cyclical periods. Real estate sells all year long, but there are some property-specific **when** moments, like **when** an adjacent property to your familiar area pops up for sale, **when** you learn that a neighbor must move away quickly, **when** you observe a property that has fallen into disrepair on an otherwise thriving block, **when** interest rates are at their lowest or projected to rise soon. Some moments are more ideal than others, and with keen observation of areas right near you, you can make purchases that save unnecessary input capital and make your purchases more profitable. Good timing can be helpful, but as I said earlier, *immediate* ownership should be your focus. The sooner you own a property, the sooner all the forces of market and revenue begin empowering you. Get rental real estate working for you rather than its prior owner.

The **where** is linked closely to the **what**. I began my business in the city of New Orleans. More so than in my early years, I pay more attention to how the city's characteristics have contributed to the approach I've taken and the adjustments that have been necessary over these years. In your assessment of which property to seize first in your respective market, consider this evaluation.

New Orleans is one of the oldest American cities, and although it has a greater population of slightly over a million residents, it's one of the most-visited locations in the country and attracts multiple international and national events. The Super Bowl, Olympic trials, Mardi Gras, and a number of Fortune 500 companies' annual meetings are regularly held here. New Orleans & Company (formerly the New Orleans Convention and Visitors Bureau) reports that nearly twenty million nonresidents spent at least one night in the city in 2018. New Orleans is also geographically constrained against expansion, bordered by the Gulf of Mexico below it and a large, manmade lake north of it. The historic areas most targeted for sightseeing are in its Central Business District and are rather concentrated. These features drive values higher, when destination demand grows for land resources in limited supply. Its port access for cruise departures and industrial transportation add to its appeal as an investment location.

New Orleans has historically had a below-average record for its quality of public education and per-capita income.[2] This contributes to

---

[2]Wikipedia. "List of U.S. Cities with Large African American Populations." Unknown. Last modified August 1, 2019.
https://en.wikipedia.org/wiki/List_of_U.S._cities_with_large_African-American_populations.

another important statistic :the city has a relatively low homeownership ratio, which means that a greater number of adults in New Orleans rent their homes than in other similar cities. Because the city is so greatly driven by the hospitality industry, there are a larger number of untraced dollars of income through gratuities that may contribute to the lower-income records, but below-average education fuels the hospitality labor pool and depresses first-time home buying.

New Orleans also has a few other odd characteristics as it pertains to our type of target starter property. Because property tax was originally calculated here on the basis of the street frontage of lots, they were drawn narrow and deep. This contributed to the houses nearest the center of the city being built with long, narrow architecture and having a series of adjoining rooms from front to back. This style of house is called *shotgun* because you could fire a bullet straight from the front through the rear door without hitting anything. Since many historic lot widths were roughly thirty feet, two identical side-by-side residences could be built under one elongated roof. Those who could afford to buy a lot and build a house had the option of living in one side and renting the other to offset their cost of ownership. The house was often twenty-four feet wide, allowing three feet of setback on either side, and was started near the lot's front, allowing for a liberal-size rear yard in most cases. This means that with the vigorous protection of historic architecture in New Orleans, a great deal of this configuration of residential real estate has been maintained.

Following Hurricane Katrina in 2005, flooding required full renovations of many such homes, requiring the addition of recent roofing, electrical, and HVAC applications, while most structures remained aesthetically unchanged. This architecture is most prevalent in the city proper and, of course, conventional property taxation methods were installed quite some time ago, inviting modern and liberal lot lines and construction. Since the nearest residential homes to the tourist areas are ideally designed for investment, the city also has developed abundant public transportation to provide access to the inner-city area, including the recent addition of biking lanes and parkways. This creates great demand from hotel and convention center staff, along with restaurant and other hospitality personnel.

The key point is that American cities grow from the inside out, and the areas nearest the centers of the cities are usually the oldest and most originally constructed. In the oldest cities, historic architecture promotes tourism and thus hospitality commerce. Further, most cities have low-income or affordable housing communities. These have better relative upside value opportunity and the convertibility from rental to homeownership uses. When you're more experienced and better capitalized, expanding your investment criteria to more speculative categories is a great idea. At the start, I would encourage anyone to begin in an area most conducive to a *successful* beginning. We all want high-profile real estate in great areas, but I'm glad I cut my teeth on property where my mistakes cost me the least possible and let me recover from them while filling in gaps with my own sweat equity.

Now the **why**. The technical rationales for real estate investment are numerous and diverse in nature. In most cities around the country, there is a dynamic range of values in residential real estate, and values are directly tied to USGDP in a subtle way. One definition of a commodity is "an article of trade or commerce, especially a product as distinguished from a service."[3] It's said that food, water, and shelter are the three essentials for human life and nearly all organic life. Here's the thing: Food is a consumable, meaning that it requires replacement once used. Water is essentially free, costing little more than creative purification for all uses, including drinking, and that makes it a very competitive business to enter. The most well-heeled beverage companies in the world struggle to turn a profit on it, and you don't want to know how ineptly most municipal water and sewer institutions perform.

Part of what makes real estate so dynamic as a wealth-accruing instrument is that it's both a commodity—essential for life—and it's renewable; it's not consumed during its use via lease or sale. Of all the

---

[3] Dictionary.com. "Commodity." Unknown. Accessed August 14, 2019. https://www.dictionary.com/browse/commodity.

business endeavors available for ground-floor entry in this country, few sectors are both renewable and essential.

There are significant differences between commercial and residential real estate, but the easiest one to apply for our purposes is that the *primary* user pays for residential rental property and the *secondary* user or the customer(s) of the primary tenant pay for the commercial rental property. I use this comparison because it helps me maintain a practical perspective for each. A retail operator occupies a commercial lease property with hopes to sell his or her wares to yet another set of consumers in order to cover my lease payments with his or her revenues. What informs my greater appreciation for residential rentals is that the direct consumer is the source of payment. Changes in business environment and consumer habits regarding a specific product aren't as likely to negatively impact my tenant's capacity to fulfill his or her lease obligations. I stress this based on your journey being at the beginning. You want the best chance of success and want to minimize the number of factors that can go against your success plan.

Are you aware that the greatest source of revenue in almost all American municipalities is residential property tax? As dependent as cities are on this enormous revenue source, wouldn't you imagine that cities would be most accommodative to that industry? Of course they are. Commercial real estate can be besieged with zoning restrictions depending on the intended use, as well as environmental restrictions. In my experience, residential real estate is treated much more liberally. Because of the speculative nature of investment property versus owner-occupied property, financial institutions associate a greater degree of risk with commercial property–based loans than residential ones, even those for lease. They view residential property a safer bet as well. That greater risk means more restrictive and expensive loans to acquire commercial property than residential ones. Appraisals for commercial units cost more, and insurance also is rated at a higher risk than residential. Vacancy rates are historically lower in residential rental property than in their commercial counterparts, and there is greater variability in value appreciation while the cost barrier to entry is lower.

A very significant component of the value in real estate investment is derived from the benefits of the federal tax code. The corporate tax shield, which is widely revered by corporations and reviled by those advocating for fair and proportional taxation, is further enhanced through real estate investment. What contributes to accelerated growth in investment is that investors can borrow to finance the acquisition of real estate based on its value and benefit from the total increase in the asset's value, not just the amount we put down for the loan. This means that if you put $10,000 down on a property and borrow $40,000 to buy a $50,000 property, if it rises in value to just $70,000 through improvements or increased rents, your return on equity (meaning the dollars you directly invested) would be 200 percent. Imagine that! The magic is that interest on the loan, which will be part of your expenses paid for via rental income, is fully tax deductible. Both city government and the IRS build policies that encourage and aid the residential property owner. Experienced investors who've established a good track record with banks can get improved rates of interest and more liberal borrowing terms over time.

An additional component of value in real estate as it pertains to the current US tax code is the benefit to those with high personal taxable income. Certified public accountants (CPAs) and tax preparers often encourage people with high salaries to buy a home because the debt service on owned property is tax deductible and rent is not. Rent is considered a post-tax expense, so people with good incomes face huge tax exposure in comparison with those who own real estate assets. Most, if not all, of the expenses associated with the ownership of investment property are tax deductible, even as the assets appreciate, making them even more attractive tax shelters than personal residences. Furthermore, some enjoy the conveniences of apartment residency and can still gain the benefits of tax protection without taking on homeownership responsibilities like yard care. Millions are benefiting. Shouldn't you also?

Chapter 2

The *Real* Why

Money can't buy happiness . . . but then again, neither can poverty.

Now for that other **why** .For me, it's both the easiest and toughest question to answer. The reason is because my answer is my own, as yours should be. The first answer to **why** was the "science" answer; this is more the "art." The fact is that you have to develop your own answer to **why** the pursuit of a real estate investment endeavor is important to you. If you get the sense that I'm placing more gravity on this subject than you may have expected, then good! I want you to think critically about the question and understand what it's really asking.

Direct real estate investing can be a hefty undertaking. It can be very profitable and very rewarding, yet it comes with a set of responsibilities that not everyone can handle. Purchasing stocks for investments is not a simple path to success either, but it is easy. Buying and selling shares of stock can take place in a matter of seconds. There's a highly liquid market, and you can buy as little as $1.00 of it at a time if you wish. I will contend that there are no $1.00 real estate investments out there. Homeownership is almost everyone's largest nonparental responsibility, and still, it's tied to one's need for a roof over his or her head. It's also usually tied to one's personal income, and its cost is built into one's budget.

Investing in real estate as a profitable enterprise is a wholly different activity. It's a big investment, even at its smallest, that includes a number of ownership responsibilities, such as taxes, insurance, maintenance, tenant liability, and often debt service, among others. While it's not an available undergrad major in any college I'm aware of, it may be as involved as any other high-level profession, and those who engage in it at the most competitive levels achieve wealth and income that reflect its significance. Your **why** has to be strong enough to carry the heft of responsibility that accompanies the effort.

Failure in real estate is an actual thing. You can get in over your head and face circumstances you aren't prepared for; some more manageable than others. Surviving while you build value can be uncomfortably hard work at times. When you own a piece of property, you own it every day. Your tenants are your daily responsibility, and while most days pass without incident in the investment realm, you'll need to answer the bell in the interest of your tenant and your investment whenever it rings. You'll need a big **why** to grind late into the night at times, reading to increase your body of knowledge or doing back-office accounting. Getting keys copied and depositing rent isn't the extent of the challenges faced in the early stage of investment.

I don't assume you will take on all of the tasks I was willing to, but I began with no savings and good but limited credit. I had to perform all possible ownership duties to make myself useful to my first investment partnership. I committed myself to performing evictions; cleaning up apartments, loading materials, and trash; even painting and tiling. My larger goals required that the early days be survived. I worked my way into ownership by doing the work I would otherwise have had to pay others for. The path was uncomfortable at first, but it was certain. I was able to start with very little money and work my way forward.

Now that I've spooked you a bit, here's a little solace. For a person standing at the base of the investment mountain, looking up at a journey of challenge and triumph, I can assure you that it can be the most worthwhile professional effort of your life. In the process of landing my first rental unit all the way to the hundredth and beyond, I've learned and grown every step of the way. I've taught myself and been taught by others a series of skills that have added to me and my colleagues' prosperity, both monetarily and intellectually.

Remember, I didn't begin with an enviable professional salary or seed capital to acquire large chunks of an American city. I served as a gofer for tradesmen that I hired in the early years so that I could watch and learn the trades I was paying them for in hopes that I wouldn't need to call them the next time. I've gone from collecting $400 rents each month to generating six-figure monthly revenues in my allied agencies. I acknowledge that my outcomes have been uncommon in scope, and I'm as much a product of good fortune as astute strategy, but over a relatively short career, I've accumulated an eight-figure asset valuation while providing jobs and fortifying our surrounding neighborhoods.

I'll gladly ratify the axiom that money isn't everything. It has been said and I've lived to learn that, "money is the last and least of God's rewards for self-improvement," a favorite phrase of one of my early mentors. *Success* writer and motivational speaker Jim Rohn pointed out that there are a lot of *equities* to become: a good husband, good father, a good neighbor, and a good member of your community, etcetera. Jim Rohn did, however, also say that if you want to get a gauge of how well you're doing, taking stock of your finances is a good place to begin.

It's hard to get around the fact that it's difficult to be really good at anything when you're poor at finances. You'll find yourself shuttling from self-improvement to life maintenance so frequently that you'll never make much progress in either. In 2019, there's no shortage of critics of wealth accumulation. It can easily be correlated to elitism, which I think is unfair.

Let me clarify something. You have no idea what the life-saving surgeries your loved one may need will cost, do you? How about the cost of medical care as they convalesce prior to returning to self-reliance, if they ever do? Have you ever had a child with special needs? That'll profoundly redefine the term *lifetime care* for you. Let's not be stupid: You can't flip a dime and have it land perfectly on its edge. It'll either be heads or tails. The result of your life's earnings won't be exactly what your life requires. You'll either have more money than you need, or you'll have less. Let's err on the side of more for now and figure out what to do with the excess later.

My strong **why** to become wealthy has evolved over the years, but my initial answer was humble. To be honest, wealth wasn't really my goal or even a realistic vision. The **why** that got me going was, in a word, respect; the pursuit of respect for myself and from those around me. I always knew I was a very capable person, and in fact, the evidence of my abilities was the punch line to my obscurity and poor outcomes shortly after college. I was languishing in laziness and lack of ambition and chose to rebrand my apathy as a pursuit of leisure and relaxation. I was going to the local driving range, working on my golf game, and all the while was budgeting for bare essentials. In case you're unaware of this little fact, let me share something with you :no one wants to hear from a twenty-three-year-old living in a $300-a-month apartment and $400-dollar car about his enjoyable, broke-ass leisure!

To add to the absurdity, I actually had a devoted girlfriend. She was in college and too young yet to identify a walking jackass when she saw one, but she soon got smart. A little moreafter a year, it was obvious that I wasn't putting my premed degree to use or headed in any productive direction, and she left me in a heap of my own squalor, barely getting by working in low-wage food service. This girl was catching the public bus to a city college while selling sundries part time and accurately thought she would be better off without me.

I found myself miles away from prosperity, but more devastatingly, I thought I was running the perfect playbook! My entire philosophy had to be scrapped and rebuilt from the ground up. My greatest frustration was that I couldn't just flip a switch and return to where the previous day had ended and just correct all my wrongs, but that wouldn't have helped. What I *believed* in my head was the problem. I *had* to be a failure until I created a success mentality *and* performed the actions necessary to have the dollars that a decent life required.

I say that my **why** has evolved because initially, I wanted to get the girl to give me another chance. I began working real estate during the day, my little startup cigar stand in between, and waiting tables at night. My golf clubs must've thought I had died. Shortly after discovering the ex-girlfriend wasn't coming back, my **why** morphed into spite. I figured, "I'll show her for breaking up with me 'cause I was broke!"

Soon after all of that silliness, the equities that Jim Rohn had been teaching me about through his self-improvement book, *The Art of Exceptional Living*, began to appear. Over the years, I remained motivated by recognizing first that I needed motivation. Whether to prove doubters wrong, or to set myself apart from others in my class or my industry, or to give a sense of pride to those who remained in my corner, I continued to reestablish a reason to push myself.

In the early days, there really was a bear behind me—poverty was chasing me down to eat me alive. Now I imagine an even worse demise hunting me, even if there isn't. Whatever runs you hard toward your best effort and inspires you to grind, even when you're prosperous, will unlock your greatest outcomes. Just remember, it's not all about money. In fact, little of it is. Of course, the dollar is our medium of exchange and the things you want to accomplish will require it, but many of the equities that my efforts have brought me, cash couldn't buy. That will be true for you as well, but even if you want to be the best ballerina you can be, you'll need expensive training and the free time to practice all day long.

If you build a portfolio of real estate, you may, as I have, house dozens of formerly homeless families just in the process of doing your job. You could fortify your old neighborhood and save the lives of drug-addicted infants. I've had the opportunity to perform enrichment and charity work for special-needs children in New Orleans through the Fore!Kids Foundation, a Louisiana-based nonprofit organization of civic-minded professionals that I never knew existed before my real estate endeavors. This year, the foundation gave $2million to deserving programs. When I was rationing my meals while managing on a paltry income, I never imagined I would find gratification in donating time and dollars to charities. Andrew Carnegie, the great business tycoon, said, "I spent the first half of my life making money and the second half of my life giving it away." How's that for a **why**? He became one of the wealthiest men in the world, and business texts teach about him to this day.

Remember when I said that my first answer to **why** was respect? That term will have different definitions over the course of your life. One of the things my road has taught me is that you don't know exactly what you'll want tomorrow, but tomorrow is too late to prepare to get it. You'll need to anticipate what will matter to you if you live beyond this year!

As a young man, my early motivation was to show my ex-girlfriend that she had written me off too soon; now it's to make sure that my unborn grandchildren are wealthy all the days of their lives. Hopefully one day, they'll say my name lovingly when I'm gone and acknowledge that the wind in their sails is still being blown by the departed Al Edwards II.

Between that beginning and the eventual end, I'll want other forms of respect along the way. A large part of why we pursue standardized education is because the achievement of it defines our authority. We want to be sure our doctor graduated from medical school and our attorney is a member of a bar association, right? When setting your future **why**, don't forget that in the act of becoming wealthy, your social circles will become more educated. When you're older, like maybe in your fifties or sixties, and have spent more time working, financial affluence will be commonplace among your peers. Other distinctions will take precedence, and you won't want to be the dropout in the group.

You may or may not be on schedule with your education, but I'll gladly tell you, I received an MBA in my forties after having achieved real estate success in my twenties and thirties. Among my reasons was that I want to be able to make a strong case to my own children that advanced education is vital and that I expect them to be capable of achieving it as I have.

The toughest thing in the world is to motivate someone to achieve something difficult that you yourself fell short of. In 1993, one of my mentors told me, as a college sophomore, that there are two pains in life: the pain of discipline and the pain of regret. I've never forgotten that, although I didn't have context for its meaning at the time. What he meant was that you will accept one of these pains. Either you will suffer the short, sharp pain of grinding in the discomfort of effort and sacrifice, or you will suffer the long, deep pain of not enjoying the things you never earned, the achievements you will never enjoy.

The men and women I've admired and respected most over the years have served as tremendous inspirations to me, and most have achieved significant things in their lifetime. Almost all of them have had an affinity for legacy. Legacy is defined as "anything handed down from the past, as from an ancestor or predecessor."[4] My favorite football player of all time, Deion Sanders, said that his dream was to retire his single mother who had sacrificed for him to get through school. He said in his Pro Football Hall of Fame induction speech, "If your dream isn't bigger than you. . . there's something wrong with your dream."

If you've got children or wish to have them, remember, when they're grown, they'll have to get out in the world and compete with my

---

[4] Dictionary.com. "Legacy." Unknown. Accessed August 14, 2019. https://www.dictionary.com/browse/legacy?s=t

children, and they will have all the wind I can blow into their sails propelling them. If your personal interests are modest, use your interest in other causes or loved ones to light your fire hot enough to sustain you through the pain of achievement. Get another degree for your kids! Let the wealth you build carve out the time, tuition, and tutoring to get you there. Get wealthy for your favorite charity. Set the example for others with affluence so that your organization of choice gets all the funding it needs. Even more practically, get wealthy for your supporters. Don't assume that your health and vitality is everlasting. Build a financial war chest so that if you become incapacitated or ill, you're not cutting the legs out from under those who would burn through their savings and credit to keep you alive. There's no decency in allowing that to happen.

Your **why** may not be the same as mine, but I hope this chapter gets you thinking about your own. It should be unique, and it should reshape itself often. Remember to give importance to tomorrow as well as the immediate future. Let your motivations be fueled by your interest in others, even if it's admiration you would like to enjoy for what you do for the world or your family. Let the idea of legacy populate your list of **why**s. Your influence doesn't have to end with your last breath, and if you really are more high-minded than to concern yourself with just money, prove it by eliminating the money problem. That way you truly devote more of yourself to noble causes. I think you can achieve great things from right where you are, but let's get your real estate wealth going first.

Chapter 3

The Business Proposition

If . . . becoming debt-free is a goal you've set for yourself at one time or another, I wouldn't abandon all hope for yourself just yet.

With real estate, what you're entering can be a weekend side-investment hobby. You may be a professional in a line of work you enjoy and that you would like to continue, supplementing your income or retirement/investment returns with entry-level real estate. If so, that's a good position to be in. You'll likely have substantive, consistent income from a salary as well as established credit. Building a small portfolio of four to eight rental units can bring you a nice appreciating income supplement that you can likely self-manage with a little practice and time allocation. Building that additional wealth will be easier with an existing full- or part-time profession in place, even if you don't make a huge salary. I'm very encouraging toward anyone who seeks to add hard-asset ownership to their retirement plan.

My beginnings were more challenging because I had a restaurant job that had a small base salary, and gratuities were the larger part of my income. Because tips are variable, banks tend to discount a borrower's source of repayment if that's their principal wages. If you're a healthy borrower, however, you'll probably find conventionally financing your first or first few small rental properties easier, provided you have seed capital or down-payment money to acquire the first property. There are creative ways to acquire the initial one if you don't have a chunk of savings to invest. In fact, pushing all your savings into a property may not be the best idea if you're able to secure a line of credit or signature loan for the seed capital on a small investment. Your savings may serve as the ideal backup for unforeseen expenses and will make your credit applications for financing more attractive.

In this discussion of the business proposition, I will speak inclusively of both the investment and the debt you will probably incur in order to acquire it. In another chapter, I will go more in depth about the mechanism and philosophy of debt and its use in asset acquisition.

The layman and individual consumers who hear the word *debt* and have had a bad experience with credit cards or hard-money loans, as younger or more frivolous people will recoil from the comfortable and even appetizing way investors refer to the word. If you're in the former camp and becoming debt-free is a goal you've set for yourself at one time or another, I wouldn't abandon all hope for yourself just yet. Over the course of this chapter, I intend to redefine the term for you and help you distinguish the difference between good and bad debt. I hope to win you over to use this magical tool just in time to save your dreams of creating great wealth through real estate. Suffice it to say that if you think you don't want or need it, you may already be too wealthy for your own good. The strongest multinational companies with huge cash holdings carry debt on their balance sheets and borrow money regularly to expand and enter new projects or fund current operations. Handled responsibly, it can and will likely be the most valuable tool in your new endeavor.

For now, let's concentrate on the investment opportunity. Small low-income or affordable housing units are comparatively a good market to begin investing in for the following reasons:

1. Most cities have a segment of their population dwelling below the poverty line. That population is either growing or shrinking. If it's growing, the affordable-housing investor has ever-increasing demand in the property he or she is looking to lease. If it's shrinking in your area, that likely means a higher per-capita income and better use and value for the property is in the offing.

2. Affordable and low-income housing values tend to be far less efficiently priced for a multitude of reasons. Their owners are sometimes less affluent and sophisticated, having inherited the property rather than being among those educated about real estate, such as you are becoming right now. Less affluent owners find unearned property to be a ready source of capital in times of financial distress, prompting hasty sales below market value or with the avoidance of good and sometimes costly counsel or an agent. Low-income property also, due to its use and occupancy, can have greater deferred maintenance, which can either actually or artificially depress valuations. This gives buyers like you better deals than you would probably find in the more attractive, higher-priced property market. A few capital and cosmetic improvements can unlock rapid appreciation, I assure you.

3. As cities evolve, improvements to infrastructure are made that arbitrarily raise property values, both for low-end and high-end real estate. Just remember that those values that start at the lower end have greater room to rise.

4. Finally, and perhaps least comfortably, many American cities experienced a phenomenon in the 1960s and 1970s called *white flight*, a movement during which cities grew outward as suburbs were developed to accommodate whites departing more integrated inner cities. Cities whose populations primarily consisted of minorities, like New Orleans; Detroit, Michigan; and Atlanta, Georgia, watched a gradual exhale of the white population in neighborhoods nearest their central business districts and commerce areas.

Many decided to commute in from farther away to avoid the cultural conflicts of that period. Those who fled a few exits farther out found lower housing costs and, with personal and public transportation becoming increasingly more convenient, the exodus continued. Extended subway and bus lines supplementing carpool clubs appeared to solve the proximity problem, but as international conflict and inflation began tugging at oil prices, the value proposition of living far from work suffered.

The story spans a generation or two, and is not without difference of opinion, but the shortest conclusion is that population growth and the congestion of transportation made the inconvenience of racial diversity more tolerable. Higher-salaried professionals looked to move closer to their jobs and back into the city. However, sophisticated evolutions emerged, such as gated communities and neighborhood associations with private security and voluntary dues. One of the products of this event was that inner-city blacks who had owned property in the heart of American cities for generations now possessed real estate of much greater value than ever before. On an optimistic note, the practice of reintegration improved race relations in some cases. Our current environment should be so lucky. The point is that there are pockets of historically affordable housing in the preferred and central areas of many cities, as cities naturally grow outward and more populous. With vigorous prospecting, you may find some of these gems for your own portfolio, as I have.

I suggest driving through neighborhoods you're familiar with and making note of any small units listed with agents. Those that are listed for sale by their owners may prove to have more wiggle room in the pricing due to a number of factors. The selling party may be in a disadvantageous position and need to save the anticipated commission of an agent. If they are price-conscious, they also may be more apt to creative financing terms that may allow you to have them carry a second mortgage for all or part of your expected down payment or for the entire purchase price. Don't be afraid to ask if they'll allow you to pay them a note for a year or two while you establish your ownership track record. It may be worth paying a little more for the property if you can begin buying it with the other people's money from the start.

Realtors are very valuable resources and know the most about current sales in the city. Call one from a listing sign in the areas you're hunting. They'll often know about potential sellers you would never come across. Find out how your city conducts its real estate–owned (REO) or foreclosure dispensations. Banks that carry out foreclosures on defaulted real estate loans look to quickly sell those collateral properties. Contact the civil sheriff's office to inquire about their scheduled foreclosure auctions. You may be surprised what properties fall into distress for many reasons, from deceased owners and unresolved marital disputes to job loss and owner incarceration. Banks don't maintain the staff to manage property for profit, so they'll often discount REOs to move them fast. Find out who at your bank handles defaulted loans and introduce yourself as an investor interested in their list of such collateral. Even after foreclosure, the bank may have to sell on the open market, and you can be there to evaluate their property first.

The following is a projection of expenses and revenues as would be typical of an affordable rental housing property typifying the characteristics of the properties I've invested in over the past eighteen years. In chapter1, I mentioned the physiology of inner-city historic residential architecture and how it lends itself to lucrative investment. The side-by-side duplex that has large square footage relative to lot size is common here, but every city has its own version of efficient, density-intensive affordable housing. The 2019 published fair-market rent for one-bedroom properties that are considered affordable is $827, according to voucher values at The Housing Authority of New Orleans and based on a national average. For this example, we'll discount it slightly and chart these expenses to estimate cash flow.

Estimated Two-unit Affordable Property Expense Breakdown

Expenses	Monthly Amount	Annual Total
Monthly Mortgage Payment	$1,000.00	$12,000
Vacancy Allowance	$80.00	$960
Maintenance Allowance	$70.00	$840
Property Tax Monthly Pro Rata	$88.00	$1,056
Accounting/Administrative Costs	$55.00	$660
Insurance (Property, Flood, General Liability)	$150	$1,800
Total Expenses	$1,443	$17,316
Total Gross Rental Revenue	$1,700	$20,400
Theoretical Net Cash Flow	$257	$3,084

Fig. 3.1

Here's a really simple way to think about the affordable housing proposition. The US National Department of Housing and Urban Development (HUD) constantly researches and charts rent growth nationally. It does this for a number of reasons, such as to help economists gauge the rate of inflation, wage growth, and, more importantly to us, set the ranges of rent prices for subsidized housing. Millions of people in this country qualify for housing assistance through a multitude of agencies, like the local housing authorities that oversee projects and scattered-site housing. The agency administers HUD homeownership programs, providing first-time home-buying grants, education, and low-interest mortgage loans to assist in the process of moving people into homeownership. When their census-like studies recognize a rise in rental rates over a region or nationally, HUD releases a new published list of rental rates for efficiency and one-, two-, three-, four-, five-, and six-bedroom residences.

It's important to note that bedroom count—not square footage—is the primary distinction HUD uses to differentiate one rent range from the next. Your local housing authority uses this as a guide to quote rents for the vouchers it awards to qualifying families in need, through its rental assistance department. When a property owner accepts a HUD rental voucher from a program participant, the local housing authority qualifies the rental unit and quotes a rent to the owner for his or her acceptance. To ensure that the rent quotes are competitive with the open market, HUD closely observes the rates at which recipients' vouchers are being absorbed in local neighborhoods. If they're not being accepted, it's likely because rents are lower than the open market is paying. HUD is likely to respond by raising rents to entice landlords to accept more of the rental assistance vouchers.

What's really great about this arrangement is that we can use the HUD rental guide as a tool of our own, whether we seek to accept local housing authorities' client vouchers or not. It sets a floor for the minimum amounts of rent you can anticipate, with minor adjustments for neighborhood location, condition, and amenities that vary from unit to unit.

Without bogging this concept down with specifics, let's just use an example. Say the affordable rent range for a one-bedroom apartment with appliances is $800–$875 per month in your city. Let's also assume that the highest rent of a one-bedroom unit, outside the affordable range for a property you would be willing to buy is, $1,000–$1,100. Now consider that the range of purchase prices of small rental properties in your area is between $40,000 per unit and $160,000 per unit, as it roughly is here in New Orleans. Using a tool known as the gross-rent multiplier (GRM), we can homogenize gross cash flow as a way to compare returns on rental units and inform our investment decisions.

The point of this observation is that rent ranges are far less dynamic than the prices of available investment units in most cities due to the variable uses and premiums people are willing to pay for prime location and certain amenities. It is not unusual to see an investment duplex in a traditional New Orleans neighborhood for either of the prices of Property A or Property B in this graphic, but notice the difference in the number of months it takes to collect an amount of money equal to the purchase price of each.

Property Cost-to-Revenue Contrast
(Assumes a Two-Unit Structure)

	Property "A"	Property "B"
Theoretical Purchase Price	$80,000	$320,000
Gross Monthly Rent (per unit)	$800x2 (Lower End)	$1,100x2 (Higher End)
Gross Annual Rent Total	$19,200	$26,400
Months to Collect 100% Gross Return	50 Months	145.5 Months

Fig. 3.2

I keep returning to the idea that your first few deals need to be very strong, high-probability wins with an emphasis on cash flow, which means that you won't have the luxury of buying a fabulous property just because you love where it's located and would rather not invest in the lower-price areas, to put it nicely. Initially, you'll need to start some cash flow and get seasoned before you take on the big-ticket items. I've got to keep selling you on seeking out hidden deals in the affordable housing space as where to start. In this example, even though the per-unit rent is $300 more per month, it takes Property B nearly three and a half times as long to pay for itself as Property A. Besides, it's more plausible that Property A could double in value than could Property B; after all, someone's already paying $320,000 for Property B, so $80,000 could increase to $160,000 while still attracting buyers. Is there really a buyer for a rental double at $640,000 when it's cheaper counterpart on the market? Our example does falsely assume that rents will remain unchanged for both properties, but I'm holding all things constant to illustrate my point of emphasis.

Now I must point out that purchase price isn't the only factor to consider in an ownership position. The ongoing cost of ownership is very important. It's a big part of the risk factor we must account for, and the cheapest property isn't always the least expensive if you're not skilled in the trades of management or maintenance. The sound condition of your first property should be a priority.

Other agencies that have housing as a component of their services, use the HUD rental pricing chart as a guide for proposed rents payable for their clients. These are often nonprofit organizations who address specific segments of the disadvantaged community, like the elderly, those in recovery from substance abuse, and HIV-infected individuals who have difficulty with employment due to their health challenges and the effects of public stigma surrounding their condition. These agencies apply for grant funding that can have a comprehensive amount set for each qualified recipient, and the housing piece of that grant amount is earmarked for stabilizing the client with either temporary or permanent supportive housing while they recover and attempt to resume self-reliance.

I participate in a number of such organizations in New Orleans, and they do tremendous work. I would encourage any investor to check out the agencies in your area that do such work, and I know you are already familiar with some of them. I was surprised to learn that The Salvation Army and Catholic Charities have housing assistance funds available for some of the clientele they serve. Participating in these programs is a great way to help the disadvantaged while sourcing tenants for your leasing operation and fortifying the community in which you invest. I suggest researching the programs in your area that need affordable housing as a source of potential tenants for your new operation. You may also find, as I did, an opportunity to expand your civic contribution in the areas in which these agencies concentrate. A great friend of mine likes the phrase "Doing good while doing well." I like that phrase too.

Chapter 4

Time Is on My Side . . . Yes, It Is!

It's not what you pay, but when *you pay it.*

The iconic Rolling Stones may have lacked delicacy in writing their lyrics at times; most notably and disrespectfully those of "Brown Sugar." In relation to time being on your side, however, that song's message is a profound and, for our purposes, helpful one. The time component of real estate investment cannot be overstated. The phrase "Time is money" is a platitudinous one with a nebulous meaning, so I will dissect It and see if it's possible to get a more literal meaning as well as getting the calendar to work *for* us for a change.

You'll recall that in chapter 1, our answer for **when** was "Right now," correct? Why is later not a good time to begin a wealth-accumulating activity? It seems an obvious answer, but I will put some numbers to it.

You've heard older friends and relatives wax nostalgic about how little things cost years ago before you were a twinkle in your father's eye. My mother distinctly remembers her first new car costing

$3,600 in 1965! That's hard to imagine, right? Well, it's true, and in a capitalist economy such as ours that allows for wealth to be accumulated, that will remain true. Inflation is a mechanism that marks a general rate of appreciation to assets that allows for macroeconomic behaviors, both within and among countries, to flow somewhat smoothly. I won't make this concept uselessly complicated or pretend to thoroughly understand all of its nuances. Just understand that it exists, and it works to benefit those who utilize it. You should be among those who do so.

Asset values tend to rise over time, and there's an enormous amount of evidence to support that it is a predictable economic behavior that we can count on. One market force pushes another, then another, creating a gradual and steady increase in values and prices. Wages increase as the cost of education fuels higher debt and a higher cost of living. The workforce needs more salary, so the price of products must go up to maintain corporate profit margin. (Corporate profits are necessary to keep equity markets attractive to outside investors.) The input cost of the ingredients of goods increases as well, and some ingredients aren't profitable to produce but are necessary. That's why farm subsidies exist, which come from tax dollars that must also increase to keep farmers interested in their work. Companies raise prices to afford higher salaries; higher salaries accommodate rises in the cost of rent, groceries, etcetera. The mechanism simply does what it does. Those costs are a way to participate in that mechanism aside from just an employment salary increase, which remains subject to an employer's whim.

There's always economic pressure on the private sector to trim costs in an effort to maintain profitability. Staff is usually the highest-cost line item in any operation and comes with payroll taxes, matching-fund retirement contributions, workers' compensation, and general liability insurance coverage on top of an ever-increasing salary figure. In an environment in which technological innovation constantly makes production activities more efficient, the layoff lever is the easiest and most effective one to pull for operators to lower costs and save profits.

On the flip side, after some poor staffers have been furloughed and profits have returned, the scheduled pay increases that accompany that corporate prosperity fuel the higher rents that will be driving the values of your investment real estate. Let's face it; this is not a victimless mechanism, but my interest is to steer readers of this book toward prosperity as best I can. While I can't fix macroeconomics, I can make a good case for getting you on the right side of its effects.

So what does all of that have to do with time? Well, everything, of course. Many use the phrase "It's not what you say, but how you say it." Well, I'll offer the following adjustment: "It's not what you pay, but *when* you pay it."

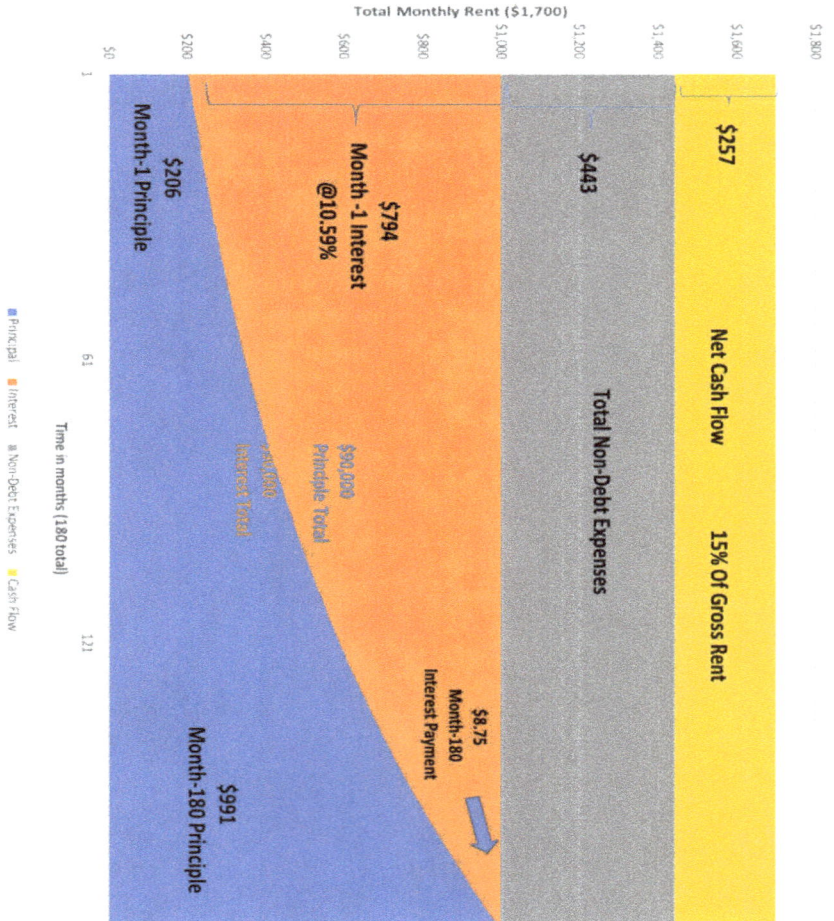

Rental Revenue and Expense Breakdown

Total Monthly Rent ($1,700)

- $257 — Net Cash Flow — 15% Of Gross Rent
- $443 — Total Non-Debt Expenses
- $794 — Month-1 Interest @10.59%
- $206 — Month-1 Principle

$90,000 Principle Total

$8.75 Month-180 Interest Payment

$991 Month-180 Principle

Time in months (180 total)

Principal | Interest | Non-Debt Expenses | Cash Flow

The prior chart indicates that the technical data isn't all that complicated and gives a visual illustration of the principal/interest relationship. A principal and interest mortgage is designed so that a fixed monthly amount is distributed between principal owed and the corresponding interest that has accumulated over the preceding thirty-day period. The total monthly payment remains unchanged, but as you pay down the principal, the interest that accumulates is also reduced. This accelerates the rate of principal reduction over time. Notice that the mortgage company or bank receives the greatest portion of its interest near the beginning of the loan, and the majority of the payment in the last years goes toward the principal, with the borrower's equity increasing at a greater rate as the loan concludes.

In this example, we used a simple $1,000 monthly payment, and, by appearance, $794 of the first month's payment is interest. The inverse is true near the end of the term. While commercial interest rates are at historic lows, I used an arbitrary 10.59 percent interest rate, which is significantly higher than an investment rate for fifteen-year debt would be at this time. I used that rate to create an amortization schedule in which the loan amount and the interest expense were exactly equal over the life of the loan. I've had similar debt quoted recently, at around 5.5 percent so the results under this extremely conservative rate should be encouraging.

This chart corresponds to Figure 3.1 in the previous chapter and breaks down the $1,700 estimated rent into debt service, expenses, and free cash flow. The major points here are that a well-purchased rental property can fetch a cash return depicted in the chart while also creating an annuity of equity savings in the form of principal reduction in the loan. This mortgage is a $90,000 loan in which the cost of capital equals $90,000; 100 percent of the amount borrowed over fifteen years. The great thing is that every dollar of the interest and principal are well contained within anticipated rents. Notice that I built in a fifteen-year term, while some can extend to twenty, twenty-five, and, in homeowners' mortgages, even thirty years. A longer loan duration would free more excess cash by lowering the payment, which in our case is $1,000, but it would make the total interest expense greater over time.

Incidentally, the term *mortgage* derives from the British, Middle Ages word meaning, d*eath pledge*. Its design, in contrast to the real expected duration of property ownership, gives the bank a great advantage. People tend to sell or transfer property long before they reach the end of the schedule.[5] By then, you've paid plenty of interest

[5]TransUnion SmartMove. "8 Rental Statistics Every Landlord Needs to Know Today." Andrea Collatz. August 12, 2018.

but very little toward the reduction of your balance, only to begin all over again with another property. This certainly makes homeownership appear to be a futile activity in terms of debt freedom, but largely because as a homeowner, *your* salary provides the revenue that pays for all of this. Although the property's value probably rises during the ownership period and the interest is tax deductible, you're working to buy and pay the interest cost too until you get to that finish line. While the circumstances are the same in the investment-property scenario, it's the rents of the tenant that serve as the revenue source for debt service; both interest and principle. If bought at a total cost that lets the rents exceed the monthly mortgage and the other expenses, occupying tenants can facilitate your ownership while your investment appreciates in value. There should also be excess cash flow beyond the monthly costs.

Before we leave this chart, I want to emphasize that the small ribbon of net cash flow *isn't* all we're working for. That margin can come in handy but it's simply a cushion that facilitates the real gain we're lining up. We know rents historically rise, so that cash flow number will only get larger while we service fixed expenses. Still, the value in this proposition is in the property value appreciation.

So a good question that one of my favorite business school professors astutely asked was, "If you could buy all of the assets of the United States but had to borrow the full purchase price to do so, would you?" The answer is, "Of course," and here's why. If the alternative to buying the asset with debt is to never buy the asset, you have no choice. Use the debt and add the asset. If its value exceeds the total cost and the term of monthly debt service payments and expenses are within the amount of monthly rent revenue, the first criteria have been met. In evaluating the decision on a property, you'll need to have the property inspected and flesh out possible near-future maintenance and improvement costs to become more comfortable. You'll also need to do a projection of future potential increases in recurring expenses. My layman's definition of bad debt is, debt that depends on your personal earnings to service. If it counts on part of your paycheck, that's less

https://www.mysmartmove.com/SmartMove/blog/6-rental-statistics-landlords-need-know.page.

than ideal. The investment debt we're discussing is the best kind, in my estimation. It is simply part of the cost of the enterprise, and will be serviced by the rent dollars of your tenants. Good debt, indeed!

The decision process has some steps I'll cover further, but remember: with rare exception, real estate is appreciating in value virtually all of the time in and around most city centers. The only question *then* is, "Is it appreciating while you own it or while someone else does?" The great Carleton Sheets, the most comprehensive instructor on real estate investment I've ever known of, is noted for saying, "You don't make money on real estate when you sell it. You make money on real estate when you *buy* it!" That's a little counterintuitive, right? But I've certainly found it to be true. You don't begin collecting revenue on a property until it belongs to you, and you stop collecting and enjoying asset value appreciation the moment you sell. If someone was willing to buy it at the price you sold it for yesterday, then it was worth it, and that value was already yours. Turning it into cash doesn't make you wealthier. It only changes its form and creates a taxable transaction for you in the process.

At the introductory level that you're beginning from, you'll find greater value in showing accumulation than just the ability to buy low and sell high. You'll need the reputation of stability with others you may encourage to invest with you over time, and especially with banks, who serve as a partner in your efforts through loans and mortgages. You'll benefit from a consistent series of tax returns to start off with, rather than peaks and valleys of net worth. Besides, cash is the enemy of wealth accumulation. Nothing generates less of a return than money in the bank. Almost all investment vehicles do better than savings accounts, especially real estate. Get that cash working for you. There are multiple means of accessing equity from real estate up to and including selling if emergencies arise, so don't be reluctant to put savings into a solid, income-generating property if you find one. Most banks are willing to finance, refinance, or issue an equity line of credit using real estate collateral following one year of demonstrated ownership and will take the property's rents into account as the means of debt service. If over that year you're able to spruce up a small rental property and raise rents based on the improved condition, you may be able to unlock some of that new value through a refinance based on the new appraisal or valuation.

I'll admit that I was certainly tempted to sell and cash out of some real estate in the early years, especially following Hurricane Katrina, when everything I had worked to renovate and improve had been damaged beyond my prior imagination. Things may have worked out well either way, but the resurgence of property values that I've enjoyed over the recent years would've been to the benefit of the new owners had I sold. New Orleans and the Gulf Coast region participated in massive federal recovery stimulus as well as private-sector investment, supporting infrastructure improvements. These exogenous events, which had nothing to do with my own restoration efforts, raised the value of both my and all others' hard assets in the city. Had I sold, I would've needed to find some other mechanism to put the money to work in. I would've repaid all the loans that I'd taken out to acquire the property, along with the fees of sale and tax on the capital gains, only to start seeking some other investment that may not have performed as well as the surge in values that has occurred since.

It's important to remember that only some of the value in real estate is the excess cash left over from rent payments. That number can be small and discouraging if you consider it the meat of your return. The wealth you gain through equity appreciation can greatly outpace the monthly cash return over time. It should serve as some encouragement that in a city like New Orleans, which suffered such a disastrous event and remains at a similar risk of reoccurrence, property values consistently climb, and the outlook remains positive for continued growth. The key is, the elevator works for those who are *on* it. You'll always have the value of your own efforts, but wouldn't you like some of those events improving your net worth? You don't need a horrific storm to create value, and I wouldn't wish such a thing on any area. It was certainly unwelcome here.

The fact is, however, that all over this country, capital improvements are always happening, enhanced by technological advancement in construction materials and techniques. Roads, electrical grids, and facilities both public and private improve, and wages move along with them. They raise demand for housing, especially in growing cities and towns. You can research recent historic population growth in your area and compare it to rates of fair-market rents over the same period to confirm the thesis, but values rise, even on assets that remain unchanged, like that loaf of bread that your grandmother boasted buying for a nickel long ago.

Another relevant point is that inflation and its rate diminishes the buying power of the dollar that your investments can hedge. Your savings aren't going to grow fast enough with the tiny interest returns in cash deposit instruments. You need real assets whose values go up with inflation as the buying power of the dollar slowly slips downward. One dollar used to buy a gallon of gas when I was a teenager. Now it buys only one-third of a gallon. No big deal if you've got a house that has tripled in value over the same period of time, right? What's important is that you need to start the process.

Life is finite on this earth, and the clock doesn't pause, so get it working for you. Get the rent payments of others funding your asset-value growth. You may find that it is a greater priority to start with a house for someone else to pay you to live in even before you buy one to pay to live in yourself. Time is not a static proposition. It's either working for you or against you. The engine of your investment activities can run alongside your primary career, and all the while, you're growing value while your property earns rent for its upkeep and debt service. It's not a certainty when you'll need that stored value to access for cash, so it's best you start storing it now! No matter what your age, you're only growing closer to an age when you either can't or shouldn't be working as hard as you should today. So let's prepare by making the calendar our ally!

Chapter 5

Buy and Hold versus Flip Mode

When a stranger is handing you thousands of unearned dollars, shut up and accept them.

There are a multitude of approaches to investing in real estate, especially a relatively liquid version such as affordable 1–4 family residential units in areas heavily populated by minorities. As of this period in the twenty-first century, there is an increasing per-capita income that promotes homeownership. As minorities grow more economically stable, statistics say we seek to invest and live in the areas near our first homes, and thus there is a typically healthy sales market for real estate in affordable areas.

There are successful investors whose approach is to buy and flip; acquiring and improving properties and then putting them right back on the market to capture gains.
While I've taken some opportunities to sell over the years, my bias has been to hold properties I've purchased, and I'll give you arguments for both long-term and short-term investment strategies.

Here's a true story that informs my argument. During a time when I owned about ninety residential units in New Orleans, I received a call from a realtor that I had worked with before, who was representing a buyer. The individual happened to live next door to a two-unit building that I owned, and upon researching the property for his buyer, the realtor discovered the owner to be familiar investor, which encouraged his prospects for brokering a sale. Because it was an unsolicited purchase offer, the agent felt compelled to let me know that the prospective buyer was the property's next-door neighboring owner and resident. He wanted my property as a convenient investment!

I, having owned the property of interest for eight years by then, was familiar but not necessarily friendly with the property's neighbor. He had had run-ins with the tenant next door who had occupied my unit the year before—let's call her Ms. Madazhell—and they had had occasional conflicts over incidents like parking or party noise, and they both tried to get our office involved. Our property management offices don't police domestic issues, nor should they, so I imagine there wasn't much satisfaction obtained from our silence on the matter.

The property was in an appreciating and well-located area of the city and generated roughly $1,800 monthly, even at the reduced affordable housing rate we had accepted. I had made no effort to, nor had had a prior interest in selling this property, but the agent and buyer offered us $165,000. With a pretty healthy portfolio in place, I saw cashing in on that property as a good way to raise capital and lower our management burden a bit, so I reluctantly agreed to the price and the buyer's presale period began.

The agent scheduled a home inspection, and the inspection company thoroughly scoured the house for hours. During that day, the potential buyer came across the lawn and strolled into the unit of his contentious neighbor and my tenant! What!?

I had told the realtor that I didn't want to alarm the tenants that the sale was pending, and I wanted the narrative around the inspections to be that we were simply performing them to properly rate our insurance. Until the deal was closer to completion, I didn't wish to have the tenants panicked about the prospect of losing their housing stability. The prospective buyer took the liberty of accompanying the inspectors in the house on the basis that he was paying for the inspection. He was clearly looking to agitate the tenant, and as a next-door neighbor who didn't know the house was being sold, Ms. Madazhell was infuriated! While already enduring this lengthy inspection, she suddenly looked up and saw her hated neighbor taking the liberty to walk through her house because he *might* be buying it.

This left my company in a horrible position. We had lied to the tenants about the nature of the inspection, facilitated an undesired neighbor's trespass into Ms. Madazhell's house, and alarmed our lucrative lease payers about the potential loss of their residency. I was sure that the buyer would force the tenants he was at odds with to move because he could fetch higher rents by leasing to more affluent families who didn't need the affordable rent protection we provided them. It was no secret that he didn't like his neighbor and would relish shoving her and her child out of the house as much as he enjoyed disrespecting their households.

Somehow, we smoothed things over with the tenants, insisting our innocence in the incident. I also kept the deal to sell intact, but an interesting thing happened once the inspection reports were accepted and the appraisal came back. To release the property for sale, my mortgage company required a copy of the appraisal to assure that the other remaining properties under the multi-collateralized loan could continue to justify the remaining loan balance. Upon turning over the appraisal, it was discovered that the property's current market value was $195,000!

The seller had been reluctant to turn the appraisal over, and I thought it was because the $30,000 gift of free equity I was scheduled to give this buyer would become apparent, but it turns out there was another reason. The buyer was angry because he was paying $500 for the appraisal and considered the report to be his asset. He demanded that my side pay him for half of it. In the process of delaying the mortgage release with his squabble about the appraisal, a funny thing happened: the purchase contract expired and now required a mutually agreed and signed extension.

Imagine the smile I gave the realtor when he came to me, hat in hand, asking that I recommit to sell my house to that ignoramus at a $30,000 discount to its newly determined value of $195,000! Needless to say, the deal I made was slightly different. I knew the obnoxious buyer would be incensed by a demand of more money to extend, so I required the price be adjusted to $175,000. The buyer refused and the deal expired. To a certain degree, I was irritated because I had gotten used to the idea of having one fewer property and a six-figure cash-out, but when I thought more about it, the outcome supported my orthodoxy.

Truthfully, I consider it a mistake on my part, to have run the buyer off like that. I could've handled it more tactfully and brought those sales proceeds into the fold. I did give away the chance to raise some cash, but on the other hand, I hadn't tested the market for other buyers and clearly there was more value in the property than I thought.

The greater part of my telling that story is for pure entertainment, but the moral of the story for the buyer should've been, "When a stranger is handing you thousands of unearned dollars, shut up and accept them." For my purposes, the lesson is that you can always sell, but as I mentioned, this house paid us over $20,000 yearly in rent. I could scrap today's deal and entertain the prospect of selling in one year, having collected another $20,000, especially if I'm willing to sell at a discount to value. If I don't like the price I get then, I can wait for another $20,000. In the meantime, I'm reducing my loan balance, enjoying continued value appreciation, and building my debt service track record with my lender. It also contributes to the profile of my balance sheet to hold assets over time.

On the flip side, short-term investors are usually comfortable with their ability to improve properties by renovation and put them on the homeownership sales market where the price per square foot is usually higher than that of rentals. There are virtues to both approaches, for sure. Demonstrating the ability to land substantial gains and the public absorption of your product is a strong affirmation in the eyes of lenders and other investors you may want to court for financing. Liability is certainly minimized when you don't have daily tenants and the ownership and insurance costs are abridged.

The problem with the flip approach in affordable housing is that rental and cash flow value is often more attractive than the resale margins in this space. Flipping also requires a set of renovation skills and disciplines necessary to attract the homeowner rather than the tenant market; a higher threshold of demand. Most importantly for the beginner is that you're going to need the benefit of a sustained track record to impress lenders. You'll look more impressive early on if your balance sheet is creeping upward in value due to the accumulation of assets. Short-term sales incur capital-gains tax, which reduces gains, and full renovations are expensive, especially if you don't know the trades well enough to negotiate pricing yet.

Further, nothing is more uncomfortable than a long period of stillness while you wait for a completed property to sell. Sales markets are more fickle than rental markets, and when there's a market downturn, rentals become more stable as potential buyers remain in their apartments longer. I will continue to encourage the new investor to stick with existing cash-flowing properties in our division of real estate. Once you're seasoned and have a solid stream of rents, try your hand at speculation in the development space, but not just yet.

Chapter 6

You Be the Glue

Don't choose not to learn something just because you don't intend to do it forever.

We've touched on this topic a few times already, but even in an account as brief as this one, the subject of *your* role is large enough to deserve a full chapter. This real estate investment endeavor is not like opening a pop-up hot dog stand with very little input cost and all elbow grease. If a small, labor-intensive retail operation fails, there's not much more to lose than your initial materials and short-term perishable ingredients, along with maybe lease exposure. Even then, there's a resale market for used equipment and very little debt relative to property investment. I've tried my hand at small retail, as I mentioned, and even at their highest, the input costs and ongoing expenses were tiny in comparison with those attached to 1–4 family investment real estate in any US market. I point this out not to scare you out of the business, but to scare you into it—into an expectation of early and frequent action in many of the fields within the business.

Just as in that analogy with the hot dog stand, you would expect to start by self-performing all activities leading up to the grand opening. You would probably be acting on the idea that yours is the baddest hot dog in the city and the world ought to taste it. Naturally, you would be applying for the sales license, looking for the cart or retail location, and negotiating your lease. Then choosing colors for your marketing materials and buying paper goods and bulk condiments, etcetera, would all be actions you would perform before the first frankfurter was sold, right? You wouldn't incur any outside cost you could defray with self-performance prior to the public catching on to your world-class product. You would open your own bank account, apply for your LLC online, and do all the cooking as you start out.

We briefly discussed general expenses in chapter 3and charted a casual schedule to make a different point; the point that less expensive rental property has greater cash-flow value than rental property that is more expensive per square foot. Within that stack of expenses are the subtitles of activities that you will need to assist with to ensure success when starting with limited cash, as I did.

Philosophically, it's a great idea not to be too precise when estimating costs. It's smarter, of course, to assume that you'll run into calamity, even if that doesn't happen. This means that insuring yourself against liability and the property against most hazards outside of your control should be done at market cost. You can't self-perform insurance, even if it was allowed. I was a heavy investor in New Orleans when Hurricane Katrina hit, and I must insist that you respect the importance of insurance policies germane to your region of the country. Many of my friends and colleagues lost everything. Neither they nor I had imagined the impossible could happen. Sometimes it does.

Should you obtain a mortgage, other nonnegotiable expenses include property tax and debt service. These items go hand in hand. If you're fortunate enough to procure a mortgage for your initial investment real estate, be aware that banks are legally bound to have their loan collateral insured and can buy replacement insurance on your behalf if you should let your self-bought insurance lapse. The rub is that the bank's "force-placed" insurance isn't designed to cover your interest. Force placed insurance is, as implied, insurance the bank can buy to protect its collateral in the absence of owner's coverage. The bank reserves the right to be the first priority on their purchased coverage, and it will invariably be far more costly than the insurance you would buy for yourself. The cost of the premium will be added to your loan balance, and you will regret being charged as much as six times the cost of conventional coverage.

Federal regulations also allow institutions insured by the Federal Deposit Insurance Corporation (FDIC) to pay and escrow unpaid property taxes on your behalf, which are also added to your loan balance to ensure the bank is reimbursed. I will acknowledge that self-insuring certain assets is a technique of some public and private entities with substantial assets and, often, capable bonding capacity. This is not a smart risk for the investor at any stage. These are among the reasons that healthy cash flow is the strategy I encourage for your initial purchases. It's easier to respect these costs when the cash is there to pay them, of course. It's also easier to obtain lines of credit to finance large one-time expenses when you can demonstrate positive cash flow.

As I said before, I was a young, able-bodied guy when I began investing in 1999, and I needed to be. I began without much money or credit and acquired my first properties in a partnership deal with an investor who worked half of each year in another part of the country. I performed the initial inspections for the partnership and did assessments of repairs that would be needed, as the set of properties were in varying degrees of fair condition. I performed the tenant transitions and enacted new leases and rent increases for long-standing residents whose rents hadn't changed in years due to their tenure and relationship with the prior owner. I then assembled some maintenance contacts to help me attack these first twenty-six units and their necessary improvements.

I took a crash course in *How to Buy Your First Home or Investment Property with No Down Payment*, the comprehensive audio bible of real estate investing by Carleton Sheets. In the 1990s, there wasn't a more popular or astute investor, and he taught creative financing techniques that minimized the amount of input cost one would need at closing to acquire real estate. We negotiated an owner financing agreement with the seller for limited period of time; twenty-four months. We put roughly 20 percent of the agreed purchase price down and paid principal and interest to the owner each month, just as we would've to a bank. This allowed us to make the improvements prior to seeking conventional financing, which would require third-party appraisals and inspections. It also allowed the seller to ink the deal without having to insist on an all-cash buyer since the property's condition would have made bank financing challenging. This arrangement made our first partnership deal much easier than it would've typically been for beginners like my co-investor and I were then.

Banking and lending practices were considerably looser then, which contributed to the crises of the early 2000s. The Dodd-Frank Act and other finance reform measures have sobered many of the fast and loose practices. I'll admit that my early years were enhanced by the aggressive and relaxed underwriting practices that banks were then allowed to employ. Ambitious lenders helped me quickly grow my business, but I acted responsibly with debt. Otherwise, I could've been eaten alive with adjustable-rate mortgages (ARMs) and loans in excess of collateral value. Those were scary times, and I know a lot of guys who borrowed so they could grow vigorously but suffered at the slightest downturn. A few long vacancies coupled with resetting interest rates, and those mortgage payments killed them. Even with lending practices being relatively liberal on home loans during that time, the commercial lending landscape where our deal was located was more orthodox, and we prepared our collateral to fit the eye of lenders in advance of attempting permanent financing.

I led the restoration of a few dormant units and cosmetic improvements during the months that my partner was out of town and raised rents to accommodate the mortgage, property tax, and insurance expenses. The additional revenue also helped to pay for materials and the laborers who did the work. The cost of a contractor to perform these tasks, initially and on a daily basis, would've cost thousands of dollars a month, but by doing what I could as a layman, we avoided paying licensed professionals the premium prices they would have charged.

Beyond the unavoidable core expenses, in that soft area of costs is where the game is won or lost. What can you do to defray and mitigate those expenses to ensure that you don't run up on the financial rocks on your way to wealth creation? Remember that in this long-game wealth approach, staying in the game lets the rising tide of value appreciation build your net worth. You can't allow a little thing like monthly or day-to-day drudgery to distract you from that goal, but there will be a little drudgery to deal with.

Your role will include responsible borrowing and filling in the maintenance and management gaps until you can build enough cash-flow revenue to staff or outsource these disciplines. While you may not have the skills to perform master trades, such as roofing, electrical work, and plumbing, you can handle basic activities like changing locks, toilet flaps, A/C filters, along with doing some light painting. Get yourself familiar with these DIY tasks, and you'll save important cash early on.

Typical retail property management services for residential affordable units costs 30 percent to 40 percent of a month's rent as a setup fee, followed by roughly 10 percent of rent per month. The services performed include showing vacant units and leasing, copying tenants' keys, fielding maintenance calls, and collecting the rent payments. The management company will deduct their fee from collected rent and forward it to you, but be aware that usually no maintenance is included in their management duties at that rate. They will simply forward the maintenance calls to you unless they provide such services and will likely quote an a la carte price at an hourly rate for tasks performed. This can get pricey if it's perceived that you're helpless. Outside maintenance firms are used to absentee landlords who are at their mercy to resolve problems because they may live outside the city where their rental is located or have no self-performance capabilities.

Unscrupulous outside service can even devour the excess cash flow of constantly rented units. In the first year I owned a property, I called a master plumber to replace a water heater that a tenant complained was no longer working. Knowing no better, I ended up paying roughly $1,000 to solve the problem. I lost money on the house that month, although the tenant was pleased to have her hot water restored. I later learned that the part that needed to be replaced was the thermocouple, which is a $12.00 item that is sold at any hardware store. It was a ten-minute job that I performed dozens of times over the next few years, and my inexperience cost me $1,000 that day. That plumber saw me coming and took advantage of my ignorance. If I hadn't gotten smarter about the details of my investing activity, I wouldn't be telling a story of millions in assets that I own. I instead would've laid out cash for skills I didn't have until I went bankrupt or considered the endeavor to be futile.

I no longer perform these tasks now, of course, but my experience lets me know what the jobs require and what they should cost when my company hires for them. That old learned skill and many others still strengthen our company today. The lesson there is "Don't choose not to learn something just because you don't intend to do it forever."

Be curious when you do hire tradesmen to perform small or odd jobs. Most won't have a problem with your interest, and few will suspect that you're secretly training to replace them! Familiarize yourself with the local home improvement warehouse. You can build an entire house from the ground up using the inventory there, but don't be intimidated. Getting comfortable with some essential sections at Lowe's and The Home Depot will be useful.

That first partnership was relatively brief, but through the improvement measures of repair and rent increase, we procured our conventional financing and paid off the seller with property values that were nearly double the purchase price only one year earlier. As my company advanced and I found additional deals, I began to build a staff rather than paying tradesmen on a per-task basis, which increased efficiency. I opened a property management office and enjoyed further economies of scale that way. We saved operational cash, which allowed me to hands-on perform fewer and fewer tasks and pay more attention to finding good deals to buy. Most importantly, the experience I had accrued gave me the certainty that I was paying the right prices, getting the right work performed, and, in a pinch, I could fill in and handle most small emergency repair issues in the short run. My willingness to bridge the gap between a startup and seasoned operation by checking my ego and performing a little grunt work allowed me to participate in a very lucrative deal that moved me to the next level through equity growth. The monthly cash flow was secondary and served to facilitate the time we needed to create asset-value appreciation, and that's the name of the game.

Chapter 7

A Few Suggestions

Tomorrow is *promised—it's just not guaranteed.*

As I conclude this little cheer for affordable residential real estate investment, there are a number of statements I know I would regret not adding due to the purpose of this book. I want more than anything to encourage those on the fence about taking the leap. I'm asked so often about how I went about my process, and I'm never comfortable with how limited any answer to that question always is. The fact is, I couldn't possibly do justice to the body of knowledge that populates such an enormous subject. I do feel a responsibility to answer truthfully, though.

Throughout this brief story, I referred you to the authors and resources that led my career, and I reiterate their importance to anyone looking to begin a real estate investment endeavor, whether it's very limited or fulltime. I've still got much more to learn, and yet I've enjoyed significant success investing in properties whose values have totaled more than $10 million over the years. There's no one way to succeed big in the affordable housing space, and I can only speak knowledgeably about my own approach, but I'll offer a few cautions that I wish I had had the chance to learn just by reading them.

Don't Be the Hare. Be the Tortoise

This isn't a quick-money endeavor, especially when you're starting with little or nothing. It is, however, a generational wealth opportunity. It's not a craps table. I've made many mistakes, but my approach was responsible enough to allow room and time for recovery. Make a sound first investment, and prepare yourself for a patient start. Get yourself comfortable with measuring nine times before cutting once. I typically evaluate a purchase on the basis of my willingness to own it for ten years, both on my expectation of appreciation and rental demand. Once you've refined your own philosophy and system, you'll find abundant opportunities and grow faster than you had imagined.

President Barack Obama Had It Right

Our greatest modern president is famous for paraphrasing the Voltaire quote, "The perfect is the enemy of the good." He would have been a great real estate investor. Perfect properties cost what they are worth. Imperfect ones cost less, and do you know what they call the difference between cost and value in real estate? Dinner. Yes, that difference between what you pay and the end value is what *you* eat. It is necessary that you find undervalued opportunities, then use your innovation to create new value by managing, painting, and increasing rent demand. Don't be discouraged by an ugly small rental because it gives you the chance to pretty it up for your benefit. There'll be plenty of time to overpay later, when you're *really* too smart to do so.

Get Comfortable Being on an Island

As it turns out, you and I live in an economy in which there are far more employees than employers; not independently wealthy or savvy investors. You've figured something out. Maybe you realize that the people everyone is working *for* are investors of sorts, and the rest of the world's efforts enrich the investor class. Maybe you love your job and just suspect that retirement will find you underprepared.

The certain thing is that there are more people around you who don't share your vision than those who do. Even those who love you won't likely know how to be supportive, and those watching you depart financial obscurity may surprise you with negativity. Seek your encouragement in the writings and recordings of those who've walked the path you're on if you can't find a mentor or real estate investment organization in your city. Discouragement is worthless. I began with no evidence that I would be successful, and mine is not a rare story either. The statistics will certainly not be empowering, so make friends with the teachers of success; the aforementioned Carleton Sheets and Jim Rohn, Napoleon Hill, Stephen Covey, Charles Stanley, etcetera. They will keep you going when you're road weary.

Tomorrow *Is* Promised—It's Just Not Guaranteed

You know that adage you hear about living this day like it's your last? Have you ever noticed that the folks who espouse that seem to have tomorrow pretty well taken care of? Outside of extreme exceptions, tomorrow is a likely event. Investment is inherently a time-intensive activity because it involves taking action first and reaping returns later, but later doesn't mean forever from now. Savvy investors will tell you that you make money when you *buy* real estate, not when you sell. This means that if you buy smartly, you capture a gain immediately.

Remember, cash isn't the only form of earnings, so continue to work for value appreciation. The guy planning as though there's no tomorrow lives a pretty dismal tomorrow. You've seen thousands of days for certain. There's good evidence that tomorrow will happen for you as well. Besides, why not work for someone else's tomorrow, even if you don't get another one? Invest and build wealth for those you love who you know will be here beyond your time. Best-case scenario, you'll be here to enjoy the bounty of your own efforts in the meantime.

Be Worth Your Wealth

I assume you will be successful, and in doing so, I want to caution you that uncultured money is conspicuously ugly. Don't just be a lottery winner and pair a low-wage mentality with a high net worth. Wealth is not simply a good salary. Do justice to yourself and your family by continuing to grow along with your portfolio of small investment properties, and keep reading. Be able to speak knowledgeably about what you do. Deserve the respect that self-achievement warrants, and grow your business acumen in lockstep with your financial heft.

We're not starting with much, so we've got some extra work to do. If we're going to live where and how the well heeled do, we must remember that some of our counterparts have been born into success and are familiar and comfortable with refinements we may be unfamiliar with. Take an etiquette class, if you must, and adopt a charity. Read up on the local politics that affect your industry, and don't be afraid to spend an uncomfortable evening at a social function you would otherwise not attend. Set a new culture for yourself and family. It's worth the effort and sacrifice to expand your diversity in your lifestyle.

Be Vigilant About Your Taxes

Again, this is a new activity in which the stakes and responsibilities are high. I've mentioned taxes and insurance earlier in this book, but it bears repeating that insurance and property tax are essential to pay attention to and to *pay*! If I'm speaking to the real estate beginner, I want to get him or her comfortable with paying for intangibles. It is a discipline that can take effort. Think of property tax and property insurance as assets. I remind you that insurance *saved* the lives of many in the Gulf Coast in 2005.

Equally importantly to remember is that property taxes are not bills. They're permit fees for real estate ownership. Clearly, both investors and their supporting municipalities recognize the value of property ownership as lucrative. Save some of your rents, and get into the rhythm of paying property taxes on time. I know people whose delinquencies control their lives. Don't let that be you, and don't confuse income tax with property tax. Take comfort in the fact that the tax exemptions we've mentioned earlier will mitigate the income tax side, although the city property tax is ever present. Cities publish property tax delinquencies in an embarrassing fashion. Don't be that spectacle. Remember that ownership is the key to wealth, and tax liens are the enemy of ownership. Handle your investments responsibly, and form good bill-paying habits early!

Try the "Twice-Baked" Approach

Another way of saying, "Live within your means," might be this. I didn't mention that I was already the owner of twenty-six rental units and nearly $1 million of real estate before I ever moved out of my first apartment. It was a $350-a-month flat near the Lafitte Projects that I remained in for a few years after graduating college. I was managing a seven-figure portfolio by day and guarding against home invasion by night! I don't know that I would suggest that extreme of a delay of gratification, but a good rule of thumb might be my "twice-baked" philosophy. It requires quite a bit of discipline, but try taking your return from your investment and, prior to spending any of it, reinvesting it. Save enough excess rent to put a modest down payment on another small property. After that, the secondary returns are free to treat as profit.

You won't have to be so miserly forever, but being conservative at the beginning can really save you grief if you should run into a lengthy vacancy here and there. It's far better to overestimate expenses and assume less revenue than you expect. Just let yourself be pleasantly surprised if you're wrong, but prepare for rainy days.

And Finally, Congratulations!

I could've led the introduction with this statement, but you've found a fantastic opportunity in real estate. I am partial to the segment that this book concentrates on, but hard assets as both income supplements and investments for retirement are unmatched for their durability against recession, inflation, and employment volatility. Few hobbies can be so lucrative, and few careers can create financial stability that can span generations without its heirs needing specialized education in the vocation.

The time and freedom produced from a well-planned portfolio can make you a better parent or spouse, a better civic contributor, and thus a happier and more productive version of yourself. A few disciplined steps performed in a timely manner can pay you and your loved ones dividends long beyond your lifetime. I credit my foray into affordable housing with much of the quality of my life and that of my family, and I wish you the same. My hope is that one day, you count this collection of ideas among the encouragements that aided your journey and that you share my gratitude for the benefits you've enjoyed as I do.

Don't forget to make plenty of mistakes along the way. Your success will be contingent on that. I wish you a great fortune of stories to tell and of dollars as well!

-Best of Luck!

Suggested Reading List

The readings that I propose to the beginner in real estate are mostly in the areas of self-improvement and personal philosophy. I believe that these writings have been the most helpful and impactful on my investing career, even as many of them aren't trade related. The industry, as most do, will shift regularly and require occasional attention to continuing education. I still consult these regularly, as I find their messages relevant in any era or environment.

The Millionaire Mind, Dr. Thomas Stanley

The Art of Exceptional Living, Jim Rohn

No Down Payment (Audio Course), Carleton H. Sheets

Think and Grow Rich, Napoleon Hill

The Greatest Salesman in the World, Augustine "Og"Mandino

The Seven Habits of Highly Effective People, Stephen Covey